Images of Modern America

MORAINE STATE PARK

The Moraine State Park office is located on Pleasant Valley Road near the park entrance at the intersection with Big Run Road. It is the headquarters of the park managers, the rangers who provide law enforcement, the educational programing staff, and all office staff. It is open Monday through Friday from 8:00 a.m. to 4:00 p.m. year-round unless otherwise posted, and also weekends in the summer. (Courtesy Moraine State Park.)

Front Cover: Sailing has been popular on Lake Arthur from the earliest days, when the lake was still filling. This c. 1970 photograph reminds viewers of the easy pleasure of clear water, blue sky, a good breeze, and a simple sailboat on the lake. (Courtesy Moraine State Park.)

Upper Back Cover: This 1970 view shows Pleasant Valley beach crowded with summer visitors. When the park opened, the South Shore Day Use Area was so popular that at times cars were backed up on US Route 422 waiting to enter. (Courtesy Moraine State Park.)

Lower Back Cover (from left to right): The *Nautical Nature* is operated by the Moraine Preservation Fund and runs on a regular summer schedule. It docks behind the Owlet Gift Shop in the McDanels area (courtesy Moraine State Park); Dr. Frank and Jane Preston (courtesy Preston Park, Butler Township; see page 27); a young boy enjoys being captain of his own boat at the Pleasant Valley Beach around 1970. Perhaps he is dreaming of one day taking his own motorboat out on Lake Arthur (courtesy Moraine State Park).

Images of Modern America

MORAINE STATE PARK

Polly Shaw

ARCADIA
PUBLISHING

ISBN 978-1-4671-2526-0

Published by Arcadia Publishing
Charleston, South Carolina

Printed in the United States of America

Library of Congress Control Number: 2016953176

For all general information, please contact Arcadia Publishing:
Telephone 843-853-2070
Fax 843-853-0044
E-mail sales@arcadiapublishing.com
For customer service and orders:
Toll-Free 1-888-313-2665

Visit us on the Internet at www.arcadiapublishing.com

This book is dedicated to the thousands of volunteers in our 121 Pennsylvania state parks and conservation areas. May you find satisfaction in giving back. Well done!

It is also in memory of my brother, Linton Pitts, who first introduced me to stories of the Western Allegheny Railroad.

Contents

Acknowledgments

The majority of the photographs in this book come from the archives of Moraine State Park. Others are from the generous people mentioned in the courtesy lines and from my collection. Since my first visit in 1970, I have enjoyed countless happy outings all around Moraine State Park, which is the third largest in the state. Especially in recent years, I have explored numerous back roads, wanting to see all corners of the park for myself. Special thanks to my husband, Bill, and my grandson Jonathan who accompanied me on many adventures, and to my whole family for love and encouragement on this nearly yearlong project.

Thanks to all the Pennsylvania Department of Conservation and Natural Resources (DCNR) Moraine State Park staff, especially Dustin Drew, Jacob Weiland, Natalie Simon, Kati Edmiston, and the office staff, including Deb Collins, for unfailing help and support. Thanks to Gary Fleeger, state geologist supervisor, who is always so willing to answer questions and steer me in the right direction with resources and explanations. Thanks to Charlie Miller, natural resource specialist, Bureau of State Parks, for the map of Moraine State Park on pages 94 and 95. Thanks to Wayne A. Cole, author of *Ghost Rails Volume II*, for Western Allegheny Railroad information.

There are many beautiful pictures in this book, mostly not taken by me. I am indebted to Charlene Reinhart and John Keck for extraordinary kindness in sharing their expert work. Thanks to Margie Opp, Thomas Tufft, Ginny Whipple, Jonathan Timbo-Jalloh, and Preston Park in Butler Township, who all contributed pictures. I appreciate the kindness of Nancy Wallace, who shared mementos and clippings about her grandfather, Edmund Watts Arthur, along with his picture on page 26. Thanks to the Moraine Preservation Fund (MPF) as well as Moraine, McConnells Mill, and Jennings Commission (3MJC), who partner with our parks. Many people helped me, including Judy Raisley, Keith Wehr, Dave and Diane Mackrell, Cory Magill, Joy Bray, Dan Bickel, Obie Derr, the Butler Public Library, and the Lancaster Township Historical Society, as well as many friends who shared memories.

I love the out-of-doors. I hope that through this book you discover new aspects to this park and develop a new appreciation for all that went into bringing it to life for us and future generations to enjoy.

INTRODUCTION

May 14, 1896, marked the birth of a baby boy in Leicester, England. The East Midlands village, located on part of an old glacial lake bed, is drained by the River Soar. Surely this baby was welcomed with love, as a first-born should be. But this particular boy's path in life was destined to be different from many of his generation and to leave a lasting impact on faraway Western Pennsylvania.

Frank W. Preston started school at age five. He knew people with extensive bird egg collections and began his own. He remembered lessons in classification of insects and rudiments of geology at age 10. After his early schooling, at age 12 he attended Wyggeston Boys' School. By age 20, he had earned three degrees from Oxford University and the University of London and begun work as a civil engineer. Drafted during World War I, he had a medical exemption, although he had a great desire to be useful. His book of personal memoirs, *Boys of the Old Brigade*, is in memory of many of his school friends from "Wiggy" who died in the war.

On a whim, Preston took a job in 1917 at the Stoughton Street Glass Works and quickly changed his focus to glass, working primarily in the field of lens polishing, glass quality, and glass properties. His boss sent him to Rochester, New York, to work with George Eastman of Eastman Kodak and his lens-polishing machine. By 1922, Preston was working with Frank Troutman at Standard Plate and Glass in Butler, Pennsylvania. While there, he developed new glass polishing techniques and worked on plate-glass handling equipment.

While in Butler, Preston later wrote that he didn't find friends who shared his interest in birds and geology. Still, on one fateful, hot summer evening as early as 1922, a coworker suggested that they take a ride to Slippery Rock for some ice cream and a breath of fresh air. Preston "noticed the significant change in topography as we reached the hill above the valley of Muddy Creek."

Today, that 0.7-mile stretch of Pennsylvania Route 8 is commonly called Muddy Creek Flats. He ascribed the broad, flat area to the effect of glaciation. Preston was still in the Butler area in 1924 when he went with friends to Branchton, near Kiesters on the Slippery Rock Creek, to do a little hunting. We know that he recognized the presence of an ancient glacier and did some tramping about in the area. He would have noticed oil drilling, as well as local coal and limestone mining, and the railroad running through that flat Muddy Creek basin. In 1925, he embarked on a world tour and earned his doctorate in engineering from the University of London by taking tests but without attending classes.

Preston decided to return to Butler and formed his own glass research and consulting firm in 1926. The first location was on the second floor of an old building in Butler, but in 1936–1937, he built Preston Laboratories in nearby Meridian. Preston Laboratories continued to grow; he added more staff and traveled near and far as a consultant in the glass industry, making important contributions to his field. In 1942, he married Jane Hupman, an executive secretary he met at Owens-Illinois in Toledo, Ohio, while consulting there. He was immersed in his business, eager to intertwine his interests in science and nature. Always a keen student, he developed important contacts at the Carnegie Museum and the University of Pittsburgh, which he consulted frequently as he studied the glacial impact on the area that he first noticed back in 1922. He asked complicated questions as he sought to understand and identify the glacial moraine.

World War II curtailed Preston's fondness for exploring the geology and glacial impact of the area, but he continued when gas rationing was lifted after the war. By this time, he had a strong leadership team in place at Preston Laboratories, so he was able to step back some from day-to-day operations, allowing him much more time to devote to his study of the land and to envision a grand plan to use modern means to reclaim the changed land.

In the late 1940s, Dr. Preston was in a unique position, as the man who had the opportunity and the means to achieve his big goal: reflooding the ancient glacial lake and creating a protected area for all to enjoy, which he referred to as Moraineland. Read on to learn about the environmental engineering achievements needed to create the recreational opportunities of today's Moraine State Park.

One

Land before the Park

This story must begin with the glaciers. At least four continental glaciers advanced south, reaching several thousand feet thick in northwestern Pennsylvania, modifying stream patterns and changing the land. Most is known about the third and fourth glacial advances, which reached just north of what is now Moraine State Park.

North-flowing streams were dammed by the massive ice from the third advance, about 140,000 years ago. The waters of Slippery Rock Creek were backed up and formed Lake Edmund. The lowlands of Muddy Creek formed Lake Watts. Much smaller Lake Prouty formed in the McConnells Run valley, south of Muddy Creek. Those waters were released as the glacier receded back to the northwest; each release caused a short-term flood and changed the direction of the streams to the south.

The fourth glacier, the late Wisconsinian, reached its maximum extent about 20,000 years ago. Again, the ancient lakes formed and were eventually released. (For further reading, see the DCNR publication *Pennsylvania Trail of Geology, Park Guide 4*, available as a free download at dcnr.state.pa.us.) Our main concern here is the end moraine, or area of rich debris brought by the glaciers and left behind as they receded, including deposits of gravel, sand, and clay, which lent its name to the park.

Centuries ago, this was a hunting ground used by Indians from the Kuskusky village area (current day New Castle, Pennsylvania), and the present-day Kittanning area. Four hundred years ago, there were established networks of paths used as channels of trade and commerce and carefully developed to be direct, level, and dry (except where a stream had to be forded). The Kuskusky-Kittanning Path ran east-west, passing generally along present-day US 422. A north-south path, the Venango Path, is generally followed today by Pennsylvania Route 528. The old Indian paths were used by European settlers, and many were eventually paved and are highways today.

Yes, George Washington was here—twice! Lt. Gov. Robert Dinwiddie of Virginia was greatly concerned because of the increasing presence of the French in the Ohio Valley on land already claimed by England. The French built Fort LeBoeuf south of Erie to protect their own claim. At 21 years old, George Washington's historic mission in 1753 was to deliver an ultimatum to the French to leave. Washington would have started this segment of his northern journey at Logstown (18 miles down the Ohio River from modern Pittsburgh) and traveled north. Part of Washington's trip used the Logstown Path. It crossed Muddy Creek at the site of today's Lake Arthur dam, very close to where this picture was taken. Part of his return trip took him through the eastern area of the park on the Venango Path, which headed south on present-day Route 528. Along area roads, round, blue historical markers have been placed to commemorate this 1753 mission. (Author's collection.)

By the 1790s, after a treaty, the Indians had moved west and early settlers established farms. Some were "squatters" without any legal title to the land. Others acquired land from the government as a result of their Revolutionary War service. William Davis was one of the earliest settlers in this area. There are ruins of an old cabin in the Frank Preston Conservation Area along North Country Club Road. As the Davis Cemetery is just a bit farther along the same road, these ruins are most likely from the old Davis homestead. For years, it had a chimney and fireplace that leaned precariously; these have finally fallen into a rock heap. Pictured above is the southwest portion of the stone foundation. A springhouse built into the hillside just west of the house foundation is shown at right. It still flows with clear spring water. (Both, author's collection.)

Early families often had their own cemetery. Snyder Cemetery is in Brady Township on Burton Road, just east of the abandoned mining village of Mayne. Conrad Snyder Jr. settled in Butler County in 1800. He was a successful farmer and stock breeder, amassing about 3,000 acres during his lifetime. Stone blocks mark the entrance path to the family cemetery, which is surrounded by a sandstone wall and is the oldest cemetery within the park boundaries. (Author's collection.)

The cut stone wall encompasses about 20 graves. Sadly, only four headstones remain due to vandalism. Conrad's mother, Nancy Carter Conrad, was the first interment in 1803; the most recent was in 1869. Many are infants and children. This close-up shows a stone placed to honor those whose graves are now unmarked. (Courtesy John Keck.)

In the late 19th century, Emmett Queen was already a successful oil man, with his headquarters in Pittsburgh. But by 1902, he turned his focus to Armstrong County and the opening market for coal in the new steel industry in New Castle and Pittsburgh. The Bessemer & Lake Erie (B&LE) Railroad opened a north-south line in 1901 as a subsidiary of US Steel. Queen and his brothers founded an east-west line, the Western Allegheny Railroad (WA RR), with a station at Queen Junction at B&LE milepost 43 and heading east to Armstrong County. In 1906, the tracks were extended 23 miles west for regular runs from Queen Junction, through Muddy Creek Flats (the glacial-effect area first noticed by Frank Preston in the 1920s), and west to New Castle. In 1917, the WA RR was loading 40 to 50 cars of coal and 80 to 100 cars of limestone per day. The view pictured here was seen on each trip by the locomotive engineer. For years, there were at least two east-west trips daily. Today, this long, straight stretch of the old railroad grade is a hiking/horse/snowmobile trail at the eastern end of the park. (Author's collection.)

Originally for freight, the WA RR added passenger service. Families used the railroad for excursions to Muddy Creek Falls and Cascade Amusement Park. Connections could be made at Queen Junction for longer trips north toward Erie or south toward Butler and Pittsburgh. Passenger service was discontinued in 1931, with automobiles and better roads being available for family and business travel. Trucks took over freight hauling. The western portion of the tracks from Queen Junction to New Castle was abandoned in 1939, with the tracks removed in 1942 for the war effort. Pictured is a modern wooden bridge, built for today's park visitors on foot, horseback, or snowmobile, where once a much stronger bridge carried trains. With little change in elevation, Muddy Creek meanders across the basin while the tracks run as straight as possible. (Author's collection.)

Coal was rich in this area. As many as 83 small mines were operated to take advantage of the abundance, with small villages springing up to house the miners and their families including Isle, the largest village in the Muddy Creek Basin, and Mayne, which was about a mile east of Isle. Deep mines were operated first, followed by strip mines. For many years, a few families maintained their own private coal mines, which were only sealed with the development of the park. The old strip mine site pictured is along the horse trail between the Burton Road parking lot and Muddy Creek. It mined a vein of Middle Kittanning bituminous coal. Lower Kittanning coal was also mined at neighboring mines in Muddy Creek area. (Author's collection.)

The Western Allegheny Railroad is long gone, but physical evidence remains. The eastern, shallow end of the Muddy Creek arm of the lake is seen here, viewed from the south bank. The long, thin row of trees extending from the southern shoreline is the raised rail bed on which the Western Allegheny steam engines made frequent runs with freight and passengers. The WA RR ran about nine miles from where it first enters the eastern end of Moraine State Park to the western end. (Courtesy John Keck.)

The railroad right-of-way continues under the lake. This shrubbery shows the end above water as it descends to the lake bottom. Underwater, the raised grade creates a shelter favored by fish. The foreground area is home to many water plants and aquatic animals. The old creek bed is on the far side of the old right-of-way, and so the water is deeper. (Courtesy John Keck.)

The village of Mayne, at WA RR milepost 27.7, was the easternmost village in the Muddy Creek basin. A rail siding curved toward Mayne for loading coal just before the submerging point seen on page 15. Chestnut Ridge Road ran north-south through the mining village of Mayne. This shoreline stone pier is all that remains of the old Chestnut Ridge Bridge that crossed Muddy Creek and is used today by fishermen. The remaining northern portion of that road is renamed Barkley Road. The middle section of Chestnut Ridge to the south of Muddy Creek is repurposed as a hiking/horse/snowmobile trail. Outside the park boundary to the southeast, a segment of old Chestnut Ridge Road remains by that name and intersects with Swamp Run Road. (Author's collection.)

Mayne was a US Steel town built for the purpose of coal mining. It had two company homes, a company store, and half a dozen private homes for the population of 40 to 50. Superintendent Frank Filer and the mining foreman occupied the two company homes. The broken foundation shown here is believed to be the superintendent's house, along Barkley Road. Lake Arthur is visible through the trees when the leaves are down. (Author's collection.)

These are the remains of the middle of three buildings along Barkley Road in Mayne. The village also had a blacksmith shop, a barn for the mine mules, and a Catholic church. There was no railroad station in Mayne, but there was a siding for loading the coal. The Middle Kittanning coal seam was 36 inches in this area. Mayne was by far the busiest and most productive in the Muddy Creek basin. (Author's collection.)

These stone columns mark the site of the general store in Mayne. When the coal was exhausted in the 1940s, the mines closed and people moved away. By the time of park planning and lake flooding in the 1960s, Mayne was long abandoned. Since the town was on a mild hillside, only the railroad siding grade is underwater today where it veered from the main line. (Author's collection.)

In the first half of the 20th century, one-room schools were common. Pictured is Bunker Hill School, which was located on the west side of Route 528, south of the Zion Baptist Church on land that is now part of Moraine State Park. Between 1921 and 1941, enrollment in grades one through eight ranged from 25 to 35 students. Bunker Hill closed in 1963, and the students were moved to the newly constructed Franklin Township School. The old building was sold in 1964 to the Commonwealth of Pennsylvania, and it was moved to a nearby location for use as a rural school museum. For unknown reasons, the project was never completed, and the vandalized building burned down in 1983.

Until 1928, Isle had its own railroad station at milepost 27.47. Isle was an established mining community with a population of 80. Watson Store occupied a large building, supplying the needs of the mines and area farms. Flooding was a problem. The yellow signs in the distance stand just in front of the metal truss bridge that crossed Muddy Creek, shown here out of its banks. Franklin Township was petitioned to provide a local school. This did not happen, so Island Independent School was opened for grades one through eight from 1921 to 1948. Remaining Isle residents relocated as land was being purchased for the new park.

After Isle, the next railroad station west was Nealey at WA RR milepost 29.68. The mines were in operation by 1917 and closed by 1930. Muddy Creek was said to have the finest swimming hole here. Pittsburgh residents, eager to escape summer heat, would stay at Nealey. Among them was Ned Arthur, an amateur geologist who studied the glacial features of the area. He rode the WA RR many times on his trips from Pittsburgh to Nealey. He is remembered today as Edmund Watts Arthur, namesake of the present-day Lake Arthur.

Farther west, Barber Station stood at WA RR milepost 31.5, at the confluence of Bear Run with Muddy Creek. There were only a few houses, probably belonging to miners. The Bear Run Mine was in this area. A siding about half a mile long ran north to the Brannan Mine, probably near today's three Adirondack-style hiking shelters. This area is now known as Barber Point, a popular area for windsurfing due to greater wind but fewer boats. The rail bed is beneath about 18 feet of water in this area, about 400 feet from shore. (Author's collection.)

After Barber, the next stop was Portersville Station at WA RR milepost 32.34, the site of the current Lake Arthur dam and the outlet of Muddy Creek. It was a wooden building with a 16-by-10-foot freight room, a 10-by-12-foot waiting room, and a 10-by-12-foot office. The station closed on December 1, 1928, but passenger service continued until 1932. This picture shows the grade just downstream from the dam. A little farther on, the WA RR left today's park boundary with more small station stops en route to New Castle. (Author's collection.)

Muddy Creek is a main tributary of Slippery Rock Creek, shown here downstream from the confluence with its four main tributaries before the creation of Lake Arthur. Muddy Creek is fed by Swamp Run, Shannon Run, Big Run, and Bear Run. These five creeks form the five main arms of Lake Arthur, which is also fed by approximately 75 intermittent waterways, including Hidden River. This water system feeds into Slippery Rock Creek, Connoquenessing Creek, Beaver River, the Ohio River, and the Mississippi River to the Gulf of Mexico.

Pleasant Valley School stood just in front of the location of today's Moraine State Park office. This Muddy Creek Township school had an attendance of 16 to 24 students in grades one through eight between 1921 and 1941. Pleasant Valley School closed at the conclusion of the 1952–1953 term. Four country schools stood within the current state park boundaries, including Sand Hill School on the North Shore and the previously mentioned Bunker Hill School and Island Independent School.

After the days of the railroad, US 422 was a main east-west highway, the light-colored road visible near the top of this picture. This is Shawood Park, a family-run amusement park enjoyed by local families and popular for company picnics. The US 422 entrance led to a ball field and the popular roller skating rink that is fondly remembered by some residents.

There were rides at Shawood Park, including a merry-go-round, a small Ferris wheel–type ride, bumper cars, some typical kiddie rides, and other carnival-type activities. There was a lot to do for a fun outing.

The white Shawood Park foot bridge spanning Muddy Creek led to several picnic pavilions. The dance land and row boats were popular. The former Shawood Park land is adjacent to the dam in today's Moraine State Park.

The metal truss bridge is probably crossing meandering Muddy Creek in Pleasant Valley. The level area was originally given that name by early settlers. Notice the surrounding flatlands of the Muddy Creek basin.

Frank and Jane Preston were acquainted with the Davis sisters, who used their family home for summer weekends. From their porch, Dr. Preston observed the broad, often swampy valley, so different from Meridian where they lived, only 10 miles away. He possessed a great ability to read the landscape and was very interested in the possibility of restoring the glacial lake that had been there in the Pleistocene era. Today, the Davis Hollow Cabin is adjacent to the Davis Hollow Marina. (Courtesy Thomas Tefft.)

In the 1940s there was a large expanse of land that was meeting a force of nature, not in the form of a glacier, a winter storm, or the ravages of strip mining, but in the person of Dr. Frank Preston. For two wonderful years, he had the great fortune to work in the field with Edmund Watts Arthur, sharing information, exploring, and learning from each other. Preston had done his own geological survey. There were swamps, clay-based farmland, land polluted with exhausted deep mines and strip mines, and mostly inactive oil and gas wells on land crossed by an abandoned railroad right-of-way. These were perhaps not obstacles but challenges that could be overcome to execute Preston's vision of Moraineland.

Two

Reclamation and Transition

Moraineland was no idle dream. Dr. Frank Preston was the right man, with vast knowledge, superior intelligence, and personal experience from prowling the greater Muddy Creek and Slippery Rock Creek valleys. Together with Edmund Watts Arthur, he worked out the shorelines of the lakes, the extent of the glacier, and the sequence of the release of the water through the passes. Dr. O.E. Jennings, noted for his keen and observant eye for nature, was a companion on some field walks with Preston and Arthur. Glacial Lake Watts had been about 70 feet higher and six miles longer than today's Lake Arthur. They identified four passes where the glacial waters were released that are known today as Alpha Pass for Lake Watts, Beta Pass for later drainage of Lake Watts, and Gamma Pass for the balance of Lake Watts. Epsilon Pass was the release area for northern Lake Edmund.

Dr. Preston had the opportunity. Central to the plan would be the unused railroad right-of-way, running the full extent of the Muddy Creek basin. The rails had been removed in 1942 for the war effort. Some of the Muddy Creek basin was swampy. Numerous areas were inactive from previous mineral extractions that had terminated. The Prestons already owned land on Whippoorwill Hill and some other tracts. However, it was far from clear sailing to acquire legal ownership of all the needed land. The village of Isle would be inundated. There were active farms, particularly in Pleasant Valley. State approval would certainly be needed.

Finally, he had the means. The Greater Pittsburgh Parks Association (GPPA) was incorporated in 1932 with a focus on Pittsburgh. Their first major success in land improvement and beautification was Pittsburgh's Bigelow Boulevard, which had a hillside falling onto nearby railroad tracks. In 1940, John Eisler of Butler was brought in as contractor for the planting. In 1944, the GPPA started to expand its scope with an eye toward acquiring McConnell's old gristmill and the possibility of creating a state park. In 1945, Edmund Watts Arthur was elected as a director of the GPPA. These people and others later worked together and played key roles in making possible the new state park at Muddy Creek.

Edmund Watts "Ned" Arthur was an eminent Pittsburgh attorney. As a boy, he benefited from family interest in astronomy and botany. At the University of Pittsburgh, he took electives in geology and astronomy. As a young lawyer, he enjoyed countryside outings with friends, especially observing birds. He was stricken with tuberculosis and spent time in a sanatorium. Recovered, he undertook outdoor work with legal assignments to handle coal leases, learning some geology. From 1915 to 1927, he drew on his natural talent as a writer and his science knowledge to produce articles under the by-line of "The Country Rambler," published in the *Pittsburgh Sun Telegraph* and compiled in 1934. He was involved with the founding of Cook Forest State Park. (Courtesy Nancy Wallace, Arthur's granddaughter.)

This is the Muddy Creek basin looking east toward Route 528. As early as 1922, while working in nearby Butler, Frank Preston had observed the evidence of the glacial plain on Muddy Creek Flats. Independently during his summer stays in Nealey, Ned Arthur recognized the glacial lake bed and realized the possible effect of a dam placed on Muddy Creek at Portersville Station. Preston and Arthur met about 1946, becoming fast friends. Tragically, Edmund W. Arthur died suddenly of a heart attack on October 8, 1948, at 74.

On April 17, 1942, Dr. Preston became a US citizen. Frank and Jane were married on May 14, 1942. They are pictured here in 1949. He had purchased some land on Whippoorwill Hill Road (now Christley Road, off of Route 528) and wanted to build a home there, but she considered it too remote, and they continued to live in Meridian on the Preston Laboratory grounds. He wrote in *Boys of the Old Brigade* that after World War II, when gas rationing was lifted, he continued his explorations. He consulted with friends at the Carnegie Museum and the University of Pittsburgh, challenging them with incredibility difficult questions. (Courtesy Preston Park, Butler Township.)

On October 21, 1948, Preston invited some scientifically minded friends and academic acquaintances, including John Eisler, to his home in Meridian for lunch and then led a field trip to Whippoorwill Hill, overlooking the Muddy Creek basin. He laid out his vision to recreate the old glacial lake. There was great enthusiasm, but what group could legally acquire and hold the needed several thousand acres? Preston was part of the Recreation, Creation, and Park Council (RCPC), a Pittsburgh civic organization. (Author's collection.)

This picture of Muddy Creek just west of Portersville Station shows both the abandoned train right-of-way that stands out with a white snow cover, and Muddy Creek. On February 22, 1950, Dr. Preston led another, smaller field trip, this one to Portersville Station, with the focus on geology. Dr. Preston was elected to the GPPA board on December 11, 1950. It had taken several years, but on March 2, 1951, the GPPA was changed to the Western Pennsylvania Conservancy (WPC) by approval of the Court of Common Pleas of Allegheny County. The new name was important. The change to Western Pennsylvania was meant to indicate a much broader field of interest, not just Pittsburgh. Conservancy was suggested by Dr. Preston, from his English roots. The many WPC board members were financial and community leaders from a wider area who had the skills to raise the money, interest in conservation projects, and legal knowledge to proceed with land acquisition. It first focused on the creation of McConnells Mill State Park, which opened in October 1957. The state was formally approached about a proposal for a park in Muddy Creek and conducted a formal survey. Maurice Goddard, head of the Pennsylvania Department of Forests and Waters, was very supportive and instrumental in getting the project approved that led to Moraine State Park. (Author's collection.)

The project had some major challenges. An initial requirement was to locate the dam and determine its height. Several locations were considered that would have changed the size and elevation level of the lake, affecting all other decisions. The land had experienced massive mineral extractions that required environmental engineering to address some 58 abandoned deep coal mines and gas and oil lines, seal 422 wells, and regrade about 500 acres of abandoned strip mines. Interstate 79 was still in the planning stage on a route that would take it through the lake, so it needed to be relocated before construction. A part of today's West Park Road needed to be relocated with a new configuration that included an exit from US 422 for the North Shore. US 422 and Route 528 needed to be relocated with new bridges. The park layout design had to be created to take best advantage of the opportunities for a wide range of recreational activities and land management. Water pipes and power lines had to be planned as well as water treatment and sewage facilities. Carl Leathers was hired as land agent to approach and negotiate with the home owners. He had previously done the same kind of work for the WPC to acquire land for McConnells Mill State Park.

Land was needed both for the lake and the surrounding park. Many owners did not initially embrace the plan. Isle families had to relocate. Isle had 14 homes and a general store, but the church was above water level. The McDanel home, shown at the western end of the park, is a reminder of many who had to relocate.

This aerial view shows the area selected for the dam. Shawood Park is in the wooded area at center left. US 422 is seen crossing at the top, with the ball field adjacent to the highway and the entrance road. The McDanel house is in the copse of trees along the road at the farm. The field area to the bottom would become the long northern embankment of the dam. Muddy Creek is running through the trees that skirt the field, so the actual placement of the dam would be out of view to the left. Today's lake would be behind the camera.

The site finally selected for the new dam was the old Portersville Station, the area of the ancient glacial dam that perhaps was first envisioned by Edmund Watts Arthur during his summer stays at Nealey. The ceremony to break ground for the Lake Arthur dam was held on December 2, 1965. From left to right are A.J. Caruso, Henry D. Harral, Dr. Charles F. Lewis, Dr. Maurice Goddard, Michael Baker Jr., and John G. Ruhlin.

With the proposed lake level set at 1,190 feet above sea level, hundreds of gas and oil wells below that level had to be capped and all deep mines sealed. Those still active were shut down. Pictured are stacks of Portland cement surrounded by empty bags for the mixture used to seal the mines. Complete sealing was important to close off pollution sources as well as to stop lake water from filling any mine or well and draining the lake. When abandoned, many of the depleted mines and oil wells had just been left as they were the last day they were worked, with no capping or clean-up. One oil well south of Whippoorwill Hill was selected to be left for a demonstration exhibit.

The Muddy Creek oilfield was first discovered in 1891. There were eventually 250 oil wells in the oilfield. Oil was pumped to a central collection on Whippoorwill Hill, then sent to the refinery. One natural gas–powered Bessemer engine could power up to 17 wells. As part of park clean-up, all associated pipelines, tanks, and pumping equipment had to be removed. Pictured is part of the exhibition by 3MJC, which restored the only remaining well. For more, see page 88.

After the exact location of the dam was surveyed and cleared, construction could begin. An early task was to reroute Muddy Creek to go around the site before continuing its regular downstream course. It is seen here running through two culverts under a temporary roadway with dry construction underway in the background.

The view above shows the base of the spillway with the outlet sluice gate on the downstream face. The beginnings of the south wing wall are under construction. Below is a picture inside the spillway very early in construction. The large tube contains a gate that is used to regulate the flow of the water and control the level of the lake. Lake water passes through the conduit or sluiceway to be discharged into Muddy Creek on the downstream side.

The center spillway, with its round outlet conduit, is flanked by two wing walls. In turn, each wing wall is supported by a kind of buttress that will be embedded in the embankments. At this point, Muddy Creek is running through the open sluice gate. The water is forced to the side by a temporary coffer dam, the long rectangular structure at center. The portion in the foreground is dry to allow construction of the wing wall.

Meandering Muddy Creek is shown approaching the dam from above. The very long embankments are faced with rocks called riprap on the upstream (lake) face. The downstream face is covered with grass. This is a gravity dam. The weight of the concrete structure holding it in place is stronger than the force of the water from the lake that is pushing against it.

All areas to be flooded in the new lake had to be cleared of trees, heavy brush, all structures, all signage, and all bridges. Submerged roadbeds remained. Generally, from east to west, this included Chestnut Ridge Road, Swamp Run Road, Country Club Road, Isle Road, Election House Road, Route 528, Alexander Ridge Road, Whippoorwill Hill Road, US 422, Big Run Road, Mount Union Road, Pleasant Valley Road, Scheidemantle Road, and Camelot Road. Where divided, some roads changed names, became park access roads, or were rerouted to be connected with other roads. This list is a reminder of the enormity of the changes for local residents, whose lives were uprooted in many ways for the benefit of recreational opportunities enjoyed by everyone today.

Once the exact height of the final elevation of the lake was known, work could be done along the 42 miles of planned shoreline. Pictured are some of the piers at Davis Hollow Marina. (See page 82.)

Two South Shore swimming areas were planned. Each has a curb and a large concrete pad that extends underwater for erosion control. The one in the Pleasant Valley Day Use Area is shown above and is the only South Shore swimming area used today. The parking area is shown beyond the intended swimming area. Some playground equipment is already in place but not the changing facilities. On the east side of Big Run is another swimming area with the same design of a concrete curb and protective slab. In the original plan, Whippoorwill Hill was to have a family camping area, but that part of the plan was never implemented. (See pages 76 and 84.)

These are piers at the Crescent Bay rental area with the boat rental office. Many support buildings needed to be constructed. Strategically placed around the park were restroom facilities and picnic shelters. Today there are 21 restrooms and 3,894 parking spaces.

Besides the dam, there were other major construction hurdles. The rock foundation at the location for the planned Route 528 bridge was found to be unsuitable for the foundation, so it was redesigned, with new road cuts on both sides to align the road with the new bridge. Pictured is one of the bridge piers under construction.

This is the Route 528 bridge looking upstream. The area to the left was the former village of Isle. The WA RR passed through here, but evidence of the rail bed was altered with the bridge construction. The elevated area below the bridge to the left was created to provide a boat launch and fishing piers. Today, vehicles can park in shade under the bridge. The confluence of Shannon Run and Swamp Run with Muddy Creek is on the far side of the bridge.

Early in the designing of the park, I-79 was also in the planning stage, but its route would have gone through the potential lake, so approval was needed to adjust the interstate route to the west. Another big concern was US 422. Prior to 1950, the highway was routed through Prospect, turned north in Portersville (aligned with US Route 19 for three miles), and then turned west again toward New Castle. In 1950, a more direct roadway was constructed to bypass Prospect and Portersville. Would the state agree to again move US 422 although it was little more than 10 years old? There had been a terrible fog problem with the portion than ran adjacent to Muddy Creek. Approval was given to construct a new road segment that would be south and at a higher elevation. Construction began in 1967, and the six-mile bypass opened the next year. Pictured here is construction of the new US 422 as a divided highway. Only construction vehicles are on the roadway. The old three-lane road, still in use, bears to the right.

A double bridge was needed for US 422, a divided four-lane highway. Piers were erected in sets with two per bridge to carry the roadway over Bear Run. The bridge decking is now in place. The initial deep road cut was taken back farther for a less severe slope. Compare with page 65 for a view of the piers under the bridge.

A lot of concrete was poured to create the new US 422. New ramps and a bridge were needed to create a new interchange with Route 528. New ramps and a pair of bridges were needed at Pleasant Valley Road to create a new interchange for the South Shore entrance.

On May 15, 1969, the sluice gate was closed to impound Muddy Creek and begin to flood the lake. The gate house at the top of the southern embankment, adjacent to the dam, houses the controls as well as the official measure of the height of the lake. Although expected to take 18 months, the lake reached recreational level on April 3, 1970.

As the lake began to fill and submerge the now-closed US 422, it became very popular to make weekend drives to the old road. At first, many vehicles were actually driven through the water while it was still shallow, with boats floating right up to the road. When it got too deep to cross, people parked and walked out on the old road. It was considered kind of a thrill to paddle a boat over the submerging road.

This concrete roadway is old US 422 as it passes directly underwater today in the Big Run arm of Lake Arthur. The elevated area to the left of the old road is a fishing pier, with riprap protecting the sides. In the winter, the lake is drawn down to reduce ice damage to the docks and shoreline. In the summer, less of the roadway shows above water as the lake level is brought back to standard elevation. The DCNR State Park Region 2 and Forestry Office is located on this abandoned section of US 422 that was renamed Park Road. (Courtesy Charlene Reinhart.)

The western end of the submerged road rises out of the lake. Notice the fishing boat in the distance. Behind it is a gap between a small island and the mainland. Old Route 422 passes through that gap under less than 10 feet of water. (Author's collection.)

A lot of reconfiguring was needed here. After US 422 was moved the first time, this was known from 1950 on as Pennsylvania Route 488, running from Ellwood City through Portersville to a northern terminus at Pennsylvania Route 108 west of Slippery Rock. For the new park, Route 488 was then rerouted east through Prospect with a new eastern terminus. A new bridge was built to carry West Park Road over US 422. Since the park opening, it has been a major problem that park visitors could not directly access the North Shore from both directions or depart in both directions. Pictured is the North Shore single-lane exit ramp bridge crossing Muddy Creek. As of this writing, the plan has been formally approved to convert this one-way ramp to a two-way road with a new two-lane bridge. A new ramp will allow eastbound US 422 traffic direct access to the North Shore, so when complete, east- and westbound traffic will have equally convenient access. (Author's collection.)

Old strip mines had to be backfilled and regraded. Planting trees for reforestation in those new areas was a huge undertaking. A ready supply is shown above. Among others, Scout groups and church youth groups gave a lot of volunteer time toward this job.

Picnic shelters were built, and new tables were available all over the park. Today, there are seven rental pavilions and 705 picnic tables. The grounds were groomed and the park was readied for the official opening. The lake reached its expected level on April 3, 1970, and the park was officially dedicated on May 23. One hundred mallards were released and soared over the lake's bright waters. Lt. Gov. Raymond J. Broderick dedicated the park.

Dr. Maurice K. Goddard is shown speaking at the dedication of Moraine State Park on May 23, 1970. In 1955, Dr. Goddard was appointed secretary of the Pennsylvania Department of Forests and Waters, a forerunner to the Pennsylvania Department of Conservation and Natural Resources (DCNR.) During his years of public service, he was a driving force behind the creation of 45 Pennsylvania state parks, and he is remembered as a giant in the field of conservation.

Three

Natural Areas and Wildlife

Selection as one of "25 Must-See Pennsylvania State Parks" is high praise from the Pennsylvania Department of Conservation and Natural Resources (DCNR) and its Bureau of Natural Resources, rising from among 121 state parks and conservation areas. Today's Moraine State Park, the third largest in Pennsylvania, covers 16,725 acres in Brady, Clay, Franklin, Muddy Creek, and Worth Townships in Butler County. It is crossed by I-79, US 422, US 19, and Route 528. Its centerpiece, Lake Arthur, is the largest manmade lake wholly within Pennsylvania. The construction of a dam on Muddy Creek created the 3,225-acre lake of sparkling water. The ample surrounding parkland has gently rolling hills and lush forest. While today a true beauty spot, it disguises land that has endured effects of continental glaciers followed by concentrated oil drilling as well as mining for coal and limestone. A massive environmental engineering achievement was needed to reclaim the raw land and water from the effect of mine drainage and polluted streams. The rehabilitated land now offers outstanding opportunities for today's more than one million yearly park visitors who seek boating, hiking, fishing, and swimming. Most never realize the incredible effort needed to reclaim the distressed land in order to create today's picturesque setting.

Moraine State Park is named for the terminal moraine, the debris of rocks and boulders left by the receding glaciers at their maximum, or terminal extent. The elevation of the lake is 1,190 feet above sea level, with an average depth of 15.3 feet and a maximum depth about 35 feet near the dam. The lake's coordinates are 40°57'13" north, 80°07'39" west. The street address of the South Shore park office is 225 Pleasant Valley Road, Porterville, Pennsylvania, 16051. Email is morainesp@pa.gov, and the website is www.dcnr.state.pa.us. The park phone is 724-368-8811. Download the smart phone app for The Pennsylvania State Parks & Forests Guide to have park information always at hand. Make online reservations for cabins and picnic pavilions at www.visitPAparks.com or call 888-PA-PARKS (888-727-2757).

This sign is located beside Pleasant Valley Road near the US 422 interchange. This is the main entrance to the South Shore Day Use area. The North Shore and remaining park areas are accessed separately via local roads. There is no one common road encircling the lake or the entire park, but the park does have 37.5 miles of roads (21.5 miles paved and 16 unpaved) that are served by eight bridges. For those unfamiliar with the area, a map is essential to help with accessing more remote areas of the park.

Lake Arthur is the centerpiece. It all begins here. This is Muddy Creek before it flows into the eastern end of Lake Arthur north of Butler at Muddy Creek Flats on Route 8. During the planning period, there was concern that the five creeks and some 75 intermittent creeks would not provide enough water to fill the lake or that water would drain into the old mines. The worry proved unfounded. (Author's collection.)

There are three main arms on the eastern end of Lake Arthur: Muddy Creek, Swamp Run, and Shannon Run. On an easy walk to the dirt road end of Swamp Run Road, it is possible to see a number of springs that flow into a box-shaped gutter flowing west to be joined by others as they finally empty into the lake. Along Burton Road, for example, there are a number of culverts below the road surface so that water flows under the road rather than washing over it. These measures help to preserve the back roads and trails. The Swamp Run arm of Lake Arthur, in the background, is actually closer than it may appear, since the shallow end is home to many water plants. To the left and right of this area of Swamp Run is the sizable Frank W. Preston Conservation Area. (Author's collection.)

This horse trail parallels the waterway in the picture above. It skirts the game propagation area, where entry is prohibited. There are 20 miles of trails that offer a special opportunity to see more remote areas of the park. (Author's collection.)

This is the Shannon Run arm of the lake, seen from the dirt pull-off at the end of Isle Road. The Route 528 bridge is in the distance, with the North Shore to the right. The shallow depth and abundant water plants create a welcome habitat for small fish, aquatic animals, and waterfowl. (Author's collection.)

Crestline Picnic Area is elevated and overlooks Crescent Bay. The sharp drop is the face of a former strip mine that was incorporated into the park design. The elevation offers outstanding vistas of the lake that stretch out in multiple directions, showcasing the lake's particular charms.

The reintroduction of the osprey was a major accomplishment by the Moraine Preservation Fund (MPF). Sometimes called a fish hawk, the osprey is a large fish-eating bird of prey. Enclosed osprey nesting towers were constructed in June 1993 for the first osprey reintroduction. Six fledglings in several nests were hand-fed by volunteers. Osprey are now again abundant. The osprey fishes by hovering high above the water and then diving feet first to snag its prey.

Beginning in 2008, the original nesting towers were converted to "BATitats" or "bat condos" with the help of a local Boy Scout troop. One tower can accommodate 6,000 mother bats and their offspring. This helps to reduce nuisance bat colonies, such as in residential homes. (Courtesy Charlene Reinhart.)

There are two known bald eagle nests around the lake. They build the largest nest of any American bird. The bald eagle is a bird of prey, swooping down to snatch prey with its talons. This handsome bald eagle is not really bald, as this close-up shows details of his white head and tail feathers. (Courtesy Ginny Whipple.)

The MPF operates the *Nautical Nature*, a pontoon boat that is docked at McDanels behind the Owlet Gift Shop, where tickets may be purchased. On any lake tour cruise, the captain and first mate (tour guide) are alert to point out great blue herons, ospreys, bald eagles, and more. Binoculars are always available to borrow. Regular cruises for the public are scheduled as well as some with special themes. Private groups may book a cruise. (Courtesy John Keck.)

This small flock of mallard hens with eclipse plumage likes to feed in the early morning and late afternoon. Here they are on a log along one of the numerous coves and inlets, showing their characteristic bright orange feet. They are a beautiful sight on a morning kayak run. For another vantage point, visit the Waterfowl Observation Area which is across from the DCNR State Park Region 2 and Forestry Office. (Courtesy John Keck.)

The small tributary creeks offer good sites for the ambitious beavers that populate the park. Beaver dams are easily observable in several places on the seven miles of biking trails on the North Shore near Watts Bay. Below is a beaver happily chewing on a leaf. Bicyclists have seen the beavers in the afternoon and evening, although beavers are primarily nocturnal. Only the back feet are webbed for swimming. The beaver can see underwater with a special membrane covering its eyes. The nostrils and ears close while underwater. To stay warm in cold water, beavers have a thick layer of fat for insulation. (Both, courtesy John Keck.)

This flock of gulls is waiting out the rain on a wooden dock. Some of the roads that were cut off by the lake creation lead to some good fishing spots; some have boat launches or fishing piers. In 2016, one dock for a cabin was rebuilt by a young man earning his rank of Eagle Scout. (Courtesy John Keck.)

This swallowtail butterfly is lighting on buttonbush near the Region Park Office on Park Road. The buttonbush is suitable for wet soils and is used for erosion control along shorelines. Although very ornamental, be aware that it contains a poison if ingested. Don't pick any park flowers, and certainly don't eat them! (Courtesy Charlene Reinhart.)

Many boxes are scattered throughout the park for cavity-nesting birds, which can include bluebirds, tree swallows, chickadees, and flycatchers. As residential and urban areas take over former rural bird habitats, it becomes increasingly difficult for the young birds to thrive. Boxes are monitored according to established standards to collect data that expands understanding of these birds. The boxes are cleaned periodically and repaired as needed.

The white-tailed deer is the state mammal of Pennsylvania. Because they are sizable, they eat large amounts of food, foraging for plants including shoots, leaves, and grasses. Their special stomachs allow them to eat poison ivy and mushrooms that may be harmful to humans. (Courtesy John Keck.)

This herd is displaying the characteristic white tail of warning as it bounds uphill. In the summer, deer typically prefer meadows and more open areas, but in winter, they seek shelter in forests, preferably conifers that offer protection from the harsh elements.

This is bee balm, a very common flower seen all around the park in the summer. It is a magnet for hummingbirds, butterflies, and bees. The name comes from a folk remedy that held that the oil of the crushed leaves had an antiseptic action as well as many other uses. (Author's collection.)

Moraine State Park offers spectacular vistas in all seasons, but autumn is always a standout. This is a western view from Crestline Picnic Area. Below, still water reflects nature's splendor. (Above, author's collection; below, courtesy John Keck.)

Four

Recreational Opportunities

During the initial park planning back in the 1960s, care was given to take advantage of the unique topography, the expanse of available land, and the ultimate shape that the lake would take. The lake's shape, with its many arms, inlets, and coves, was not chosen by man except as an outcome of the placement of the dam and the resulting size and elevation of the lake. If the dam had been placed just east of Isle, the resulting lake would have only impounded Muddy Creek, Swamp Run, and Shannon Run and been rather small. To create a park with true regional appeal, the goal was to take full advantage of the glacial plain and create a park with dynamic potential for recreation and outdoor environmental study. Any size lake in that basin would have involved dealing with major land reclamation issues. It was right and proper to deal with the pollution on the larger scale, with reclaimed land preserved for future generations. Lake Arthur is eight miles in length.

Those who only visit in the summer may not think about activities in other seasons, but the park offers winter activities and beautiful snow-covered scenes. It must be noted that the park does not monitor the thickness of the lake ice; visitors must use caution if going out onto the ice. Thickness can vary widely on any given day in different areas due to depth, sun or shade, flowing water beneath the surface, wind chill differences, and other variables. Winterfest is typically held in January or February and is organized by the Moraine Preservation Fund. There are vendors, demonstrations, competitions, and fun!

What could be better weather for a winter festival than enough snow on a cold but calm, sunny day? These folks are registering for the snowshoe hike. Below, one of several ice sculptures is being created. Afterwards, the ice sculptures are moved to outside the park office, where they can be enjoyed by all for as long as the temperature allows. The festival features a very popular chili cook-off. See the MPF website for details. (Both, courtesy Charlene Reinhart.)

This ice-fishing demonstration is conducted right by the frozen lake. It is a good introduction to the sport given by those experienced in this specialized activity. See the MPF website for more details about all Winterfest activities. (Courtesy Charlene Reinhart.)

The next activities are not part of Winterfest but can be seen any time there has been an extended hard freeze. Ice-fishing requires some specialized equipment and attention to safety. Here, an ice auger is used to drill through the ice. (Courtesy Charlene Reinhart.)

With the wind whipping across the ice, it is essential to be prepared for the cold. This fisherman has outerwear for cold temperatures, boots, gloves, and a collapsible shelter. It is possible to get out of the wind with the hole in the ice right in the shelter. Notice the brick Zion Baptist Church to the left and the Route 528 bridge in the background, as well as other people fishing on the ice. The large green hut in the right background can accommodate more than one or provide room for gear. Both of the fishermen below did well this trip. Their faces show that it was all worth it. (All, courtesy Charlene Reinhart.)

Anybody ready to try kite skiing on the frozen lake? Some hearty souls prefer the challenge of ice boating. (Both, courtesy Charlene Reinhart.)

Conditions and timing had to be just right for this park activity. The Sunken Garden Trail had enough snow for cross-country skiing, the weather looked reliable a few days ahead, and there was a ready supply of luminaria that had been prepared by a local service organization but were unused due to rain on Christmas Eve. An announcement was made on Facebook (Friends of Moraine State Park) that offered evening cross-country skiing that weekend. Happily, a great group of enthusiasts responded and attended the special experience of evening skiing, enjoying the luminaria set out along the trail and a big welcoming fire pit. (Courtesy Charlene Reinhart.)

Dog sledding? Why not. The day is clear, the snow is not too deep, and this team is ready. Below, the seven-mile paved bike trail is favored by many who enjoy winter walks when the snow is light, not deep, and the day is not too cold. Since it follows the North Shore, there are some easy parking areas that are relatively flat and close to the trail access points, making a winter walk a pleasure. Use caution, since snowmobiles may also use the same trail when there is at least six inches of snow. (Above, courtesy Charlene Reinhart; below, author's collection.)

This winter view shows the small inlet on the North Shore of Lake Arthur between Watts Bay and Davis Hollow Marina. There is a convenient parking lot on the one-way portion of North Shore Drive to safely access the bike trail. It is a good example of how a winter view can be much different than the same spot in the summer. All that brush in the foreground would be covered in leaves, perhaps blocking the view of the water. But a winter's day shows magical ice. (Courtesy Margie Opp.)

This beaver dam is along the North Shore bike trail. Beavers do not hibernate, but prepare for winter by storing a pile of sticks and logs from younger trees under the water for a stock of food. The wetlands that result from the beavers' work create habitats for other animals. With the leaves down, a winter walk can reveal many sights hidden by summer's foliage. (Courtesy Margie Opp.)

Moraine State Park has six trails that are blazed and receive some maintenance. Each is described on the park map. When finished, the North Country National Scenic Trail will cover 4,600 miles from New York to North Dakota. The Moraine segment covers 14.8 miles and links with a segment coming from McConnells Mill State Park to the southwest and Jennings Environmental Education Center to the northeast. The trail, marked with blue blazes, crosses streams and has vistas of Lake Arthur as it winds through forests. The Link Road shelter is available to backpackers by reservation only. The Glacial Ridge Trail is rated "most difficult" and is designated as part of the North County Trail. (Author's collection.)

The North Country Trail passes beneath the western end of the US 422 bridge as it spans the Bear Run arm of Lake Arthur. It is a good example of how some special views are only accessible by hiking the trails. (Author's collection.)

The morning fog creates a special atmosphere. Above, the west end of the US 422 bridge is just visible through the fog in the early light. Below, a nearby bench makes this a special place for solitude or for a rest for North Country Trail hikers. This is very close to old Portersville Station, the location of today's Lake Arthur dam.

Here is another view that is only seen from the North Country Trail: the downstream face of the Lake Arthur dam. There is a bench along the path to rest and enjoy this view. The brick gatehouse, clearly seen here, controls the water flow, which is usually only adjusted in the late fall to draw down the lake level and again in the spring to raise it to the normal level. The exit sluice gate at the bottom of the spillway can be seen here. Stacked stones protect the banks. Water only goes over the spillway when the lake level is that high. (Courtesy Charlene Reinhart.)

A recent addition to the North Country Trail is an aluminum bridge that spans Muddy Creek in the Shawood Park area, possibly the site of the old white wooden bridge to the Shawood Park Picnic Area. It is very near the cement pad remains of the old skating rink. This new crossing is upstream from the bridge on the North Shore ramp, which previously was used by hikers to cross Muddy Creek. Visitors looking for an interesting hike on a segment of the North Country Trail might park at McDanels, pick up the trail where it crosses McDanel Road, and head south to the sites described above. (Author's collection.)

The bike rental parking lot is another convenient place to pick up the North Country Trail. Nearby, it crosses the wooden foot bridge over Hidden River. Notice the blue blaze on the right handrail. This is the same part of the trail used by hikers on the First Day Hike on New Year's Day. A small side trail just before the steps gives an overlook of the Hidden River area favored by kayakers and the outcrop of Vanport limestone. (Courtesy John Keck.)

This park trail, covering Whippoorwill Hill from Route 528 to Park Road, was named by Dr. Frank Preston in honor of his English school classmates at Wyggeston Boys' School. The Prestons owned property on Whippoorwill Hill and donated it to the Western Pennsylvania Conservancy as an early part of land acquisition. Wyggeston Trail is rated "most difficult." (Author's collection.)

Hilltop Trail offers "more difficult" hiking. The trail has flat grassy areas as well as inclines to views high above the highway and the lake. There is a parking lot at the trailhead. Nearby, adjacent to the Pleasant View Picnic Area, is a popular hill for sledding in the winter. (Author's collection.)

The Pleasant Valley Trail is rated "easiest hiking," passing through the hills and valleys of the South Shore. When conditions permit, the trail is groomed for cross-country skiing. Access is from the Pleasant Valley Picnic Area. The picture below shows the author on the trail with a trusty hiking stick. (Left, author's collection; below, courtesy Jonathan Timbo-Jalloh.)

This is Sunken Garden Trail, which offers views of the lake shoreline and varied habitats. It is also accessed from Pleasant Valley Picnic Area and is rated "easiest hiking," with some moderate inclines. The trail is groomed for cross-country skiing when conditions permit. (Courtesy Jonathan Timbo-Jalloh.)

Moraine State Park offers rental cabins year-round in a colony in the Five Points area in the northwest section of the park, accessed by North Shore Drive. The cabins have a 90-percent occupancy rate, second highest of Pennsylvania state parks; reservations are a must. Five Points Trail offers "easiest hiking." It meanders through forests, by a small pond, and near Lakeview Beach and the cabin colony. (Author's collection.)

These stairs lead directly from a cabin to the dock. Each of the 11 cabins has its own dock along a more secluded inlet with direct access to the lake. Cabins have electric heat, two bedrooms, a bathroom with a shower, a kitchen, and living/dining area, and sleep six. Organized groups can make reservations for tent camping at Muskrat Cove or Five Points rustic sites with picnic tables, cooking grills, and water, but no showers. (Left, author's collection; below, courtesy Charlene Reinhart.)

This fisherman found a quiet spot along the shore of the Bear Run arm of the lake. With 42 miles of shoreline, there may be some competition for certain popular spots, but isolated spots are available to everyone. (Courtesy Charlene Reinhart.)

Lake Arthur is a warm-water fishery. Common species are northern pike, largemouth bass, channel catfish, black crappie, and bluegill. Muskellunge, walleye, and hybrid striped bass are stocked. Fish habitat structures are installed throughout the lake. Check the park map for regulations and ADA-accessible fishing pier locations. (Courtesy John Keck.)

These fishermen seem to enjoy the solitude found in a quiet cove or inlet along the 42-mile shore. Fishing enthusiasts frequently do not like to share the location of their favorite spot. (Both, courtesy John Keck.)

This man is having a great time with his remote-control speed boat as a motor boat passes in the distance. There is plenty of room for every enjoyment. Lake Arthur has a 20-horsepower limit. (Courtesy Charlene Reinhart.)

Stand up paddle boarding is currently popular. An off-shoot of ocean surfing, many enjoy it for sightseeing or fitness. (Courtesy Charlene Reinhart.)

These women prefer to do their yoga on a paddleboard, stabilized by a friend standing in the water. Watch Facebook for postings by Friends of Moraine State Park for yoga on the beach. Enjoy birds singing, water lapping, and canoes passing, all while sitting in complete relaxation. Or perhaps enjoy a stargazing party, a full-moon paddle, or Tag a Monarch Day. (Courtesy Charlene Reinhart.)

These small sailboats are pulled up on the shore at Pleasant Valley, ready for use during a regatta. Some simple training is offered by experienced sailors to let folks have a new experience. Notice the open area in the background across the lake. That is the planned swimming area mentioned on page 36 that was never developed. (Courtesy Margie Opp.)

Lake Arthur has nine public boat launches. The three marinas are Crescent Bay, Watts Bay, and Davis Hollow. Sailing conditions are ideal. There are races and sailing instruction classes during the summer. Colorful sails do catch the eye. (Above, courtesy John Keck; below, courtesy Charlene Reinhart.)

Kayak groups offer instructional clinics. Park staff offer organized kayak experiences on the water. Hidden River is popular for this, because the water is calmer. (Courtesy Charlene Reinhart.)

This young kayaker had some instruction as part of a Scouting experience. He is wearing his helmet and life vest and is in the right size kayak for him. His look of determination shows his eagerness to practice his new skills.

A kayak can be the best way to explore the small inlets and waterways that feed into the lake. Quietly paddling is peaceful and brings one close to nature. The view below is another that is best captured from a kayak. It shows the northern end of so-called Snake Island (due to its shape). It is between the access to Hidden River and Five Points, just east of the dam. (Both, courtesy John Keck.)

It is wise for the more inexperienced to stay together with experienced leaders. This group is in Hidden River, along the exposed Vanport limestone wall. (Courtesy Charlene Reinhart.)

Limestone was heavily quarried and shipped out daily on the Western Allegheny Railroad in the early part of the 20th century. Fortunately, this area is open for enjoyment today. (Courtesy John Keck.)

At Watts Bay Marina on the North Shore, a numbered space for dry mooring may be rented to store privately owned boats that can be launched right there. The marina can accommodate 138 boats, including tie downs, and 36 small sailboats and sailboards in rack spaces. (Courtesy Charlene Reinhart.)

Davis Hollow Marina has seasonal mooring for almost 700 vessels, including sailboats, catamarans, motorboats, and pontoon boats, plus canoe racks and dry mooring room for 80. A sanitary dump station is available only for tenants. (Courtesy Charlene Reinhart.)

Here's the same marina from the lake view. Compare to the view on page 35 of this marina before the lake was filled. (Courtesy John Keck.)

Disk golf is available on the North Shore. There is an 18-hole course in the Lakeview Day Use Area. The Pittsburgh Flying Disc Society was integral in establishing the course. The enthusiast group has sponsored championship events here. (Courtesy Charlene Reinhart.)

There are equestrian trails on the southwest and east sides of the park. Riding is limited to designated trails. The map shows parking lot access points for each trail. When the park was in the planning stage, some roads that would be cut off by the lake were repurposed into trails for hiking, horseback riding, and snowmobiles. (Courtesy Charlene Reinhart.)

Once—just once—a year, the gates are opened and Jeeps are allowed on certain trails. Nearby Butler is the recognized home of the Jeep. The vehicle was invented in 1940 by the Bantam Motor Car Company in response to the Army's call for an all-purpose vehicle for World War II, although the production contract was let elsewhere. A local Jeep enthusiast group hosts a yearly festival at a nearby campground. On that weekend, they may drive their Jeeps on certain trails as part of the festival activities. (Courtesy Charlene Reinhart.)

This picture, taken around 1970 when the park opened, shows the curb and cement pad that extends out into the water in the Pleasant Valley Day Use Area. This was installed before the lake was flooded, since the exact elevation for the finished lake was known. Compare with page 36.

Sometimes the park is a wonderful place to sit quietly with a good book. Many people find it relaxing to be away from technology. This picture is from the John Eisler Picnic Grove, at the eastern end of Crestline Picnic Area on the hill overlooking Crescent Bay. (Author's collection.)

Five

Education, Projects, and Special Events

Moraine State Park is a kind of second home to a wide range of people who feel a strong attachment to varying aspects of the park, such as the recreational opportunities, geology, history, formalized skill training, kids' opportunities, scenic beauty, competitions, socialization, or escape for solitude. Many serve as volunteers and give time to help with the operation of the park and support the vast opportunities.

Park partners support the park in different ways. The Moraine Preservation Fund is by far the largest, with a mission of promoting community stewardship of natural resources within Moraine and McConnells Mill State Parks and Jennings Environmental Education Center. It offers educational programs for the public, operates the *Nautical Nature* pontoon boat and the Owlet Gift Shop, and carries out dynamic projects such as the osprey reintroduction. See the MPF website (www.morainepreservationfund.org) for a full description.

The Moraine, McConnells Mill, and Jennings Commission (3MJC) is dedicated to providing valuable information to park visitors and carrying out projects that promote stewardship of valuable natural resources. Volunteers with 3MJC operate the restored oil well No. 19. Removing invasive species and promoting native plants is an ongoing project. They target a specific area on a certain day to physically pull out the invaders that crowd out native plants. They have monthly meetings with informative programs. See their website (3mjc.org) for the oil field demonstration day schedule and more about invasive species.

The Butler County chapter of the North Country Trail is dedicated to the care of the trail as it passes through Butler County, so it has contact with the park as it cares for the 14 miles of the trail that transverse the park.

Special-interest groups sponsor events at the park, such as running events, bike races, and workshops in winter skiing or boating skills. The DCNR staff of Moraine State Park provide programs for children and adults in a wide range of interesting topics. Programs for the public are advertised and posted in a full schedule on the DCNR website under the calendar of events. Others are taken into schools or to groups by special arrangement.

There are four concessions operated in the park by outside vendors. Food concessions are available seasonally at Pleasant Valley and Lakeview beach areas. Bikes can be rented at the building on North Shore Drive, near the entrance from West Park Road. A boat concession rents a variety of boats at Crescent Bay on the South Shore. The Moraine Outdoor Center is a park building that is available for rent for special events with a grand view of the lake. Some park programs, trainings, and other meetings are held there. It is adjacent to the Davis Hollow Marina. Call the park office for information. The Owlet Gift Shop is operated by the Moraine Preservation Fund and is located in the McDanels Area.

DCNR environmental education specialists offer school programs for students on field trips as well as summer programs. A park environmental educational specialist leads a summer DiscoverE day camp. Here, children are learning about the raccoon using this kid-friendly version. This kind of organized experience helps young children to learn and explore nature in a safe setting. Below, some "Hide N Seekers" are making tracks in another early childhood park program for children ages four to five and their parents.

These older children are part of this DiscoverE day camp. They are quietly observing a deer as they learn about animal traces.

A wounded warriors group hosts various events at Moraine State Park that are part of morale building. These warriors are participating in a cycling event. (Courtesy Charlene Reinhart.)

Muddy Creek Oil Well No. 19 has been restored with its Bessemer gas engine and oil well equipment at the Marshall-Barr site. It was first operated for the Lake Arthur Regatta in August 2000. The Muddy Creek Oil Well site volunteers received the 2005 DCNR annual award, which is granted each year for restoring a site and developing it into a valued state park attraction. The historic oil exhibit is accessed via Park Road. It operates at scheduled times during the summer. Below is the engine plaque. (Both, Author's collection.)

The Lake Arthur Regatta is held annually in August, featuring two days of entertainment. The main stage is a focal point with a hillside of great seating. Several rows of tents house vendors, food, information booths, and participation opportunities. There are lots of activities in the water. Try yoga on the shore in the morning, sailing in the afternoon, or the car cruise. (Courtesy Margie Opp.)

The National Boy Scout Jamboree was held at Moraine State Park in 1973 and 1977. There were encampments all over the park. Pictured is the Skill-O-Rama. The sandy Lakeshore swimming area was added for the Scouts' use at the 1973 event. To facilitate the heavy traffic, a temporary northbound interchange was opened on I-79, but it was bulldozed closed afterwards. It is still visible on satellite maps, near the bike rental office.

In 2010, Boy Scout Campaganza was held on a regional level. This aerial view of Pleasant Valley shows encampments. There were skill lessons and friendly competitions.

In 1959, the General Assembly of Pennsylvania enacted House Bill 2386, authorizing $1 million for the acquisition of lands for Western Pennsylvania park development. John Eisler of Butler immediately organized a meeting in Harrisburg and traveled there with a persuasive group of local leaders to make it plain that "The people of Butler County want the lake in the Muddy Creek valley." Their case was strong, and $250,000 was approved. The Muddy Creek plan could officially move forward. Today, the John M. Eisler Picnic Grove sits prominently at the eastern end of Crestline Picnic Area, with commanding views of the lake in all directions. Eisler's leadership and continued involvement with both McConnells Mill and Moraine State Parks helped to make them a reality. (Above, author's collection.)

After Dr. Preston's death in 1989, a large area at the eastern end of the park was designated the Frank W. Preston Conservation Area. It is a fitting tribute to the man and his vision. In her will, his widow, Jane Preston, who died in 2008, left their 88-acre estate, including the laboratory, to Butler Township. It is listed in the National Register of Historic Places and is now open to the public as Preston Park. (Author's collection.)

At the dedication of Lake Arthur and Moraine State Park, Dr. Preston referred to the legend of King Arthur. The King's sword, Excalibur, was given to him by the Lady of the Lake. Merlin the magician instructed King Arthur to keep the sword until he was dying. At that point, he gave it to Sir Belvedere with instructions to cast it forth. The Lady of the Lake rose to receive it back again. Ned Arthur's geologic hammer was always with him until he died in 1948, and then it passed to Dr. Preston, who carried it always in his car. Preston had "Excalibur" engraved on the hammer.

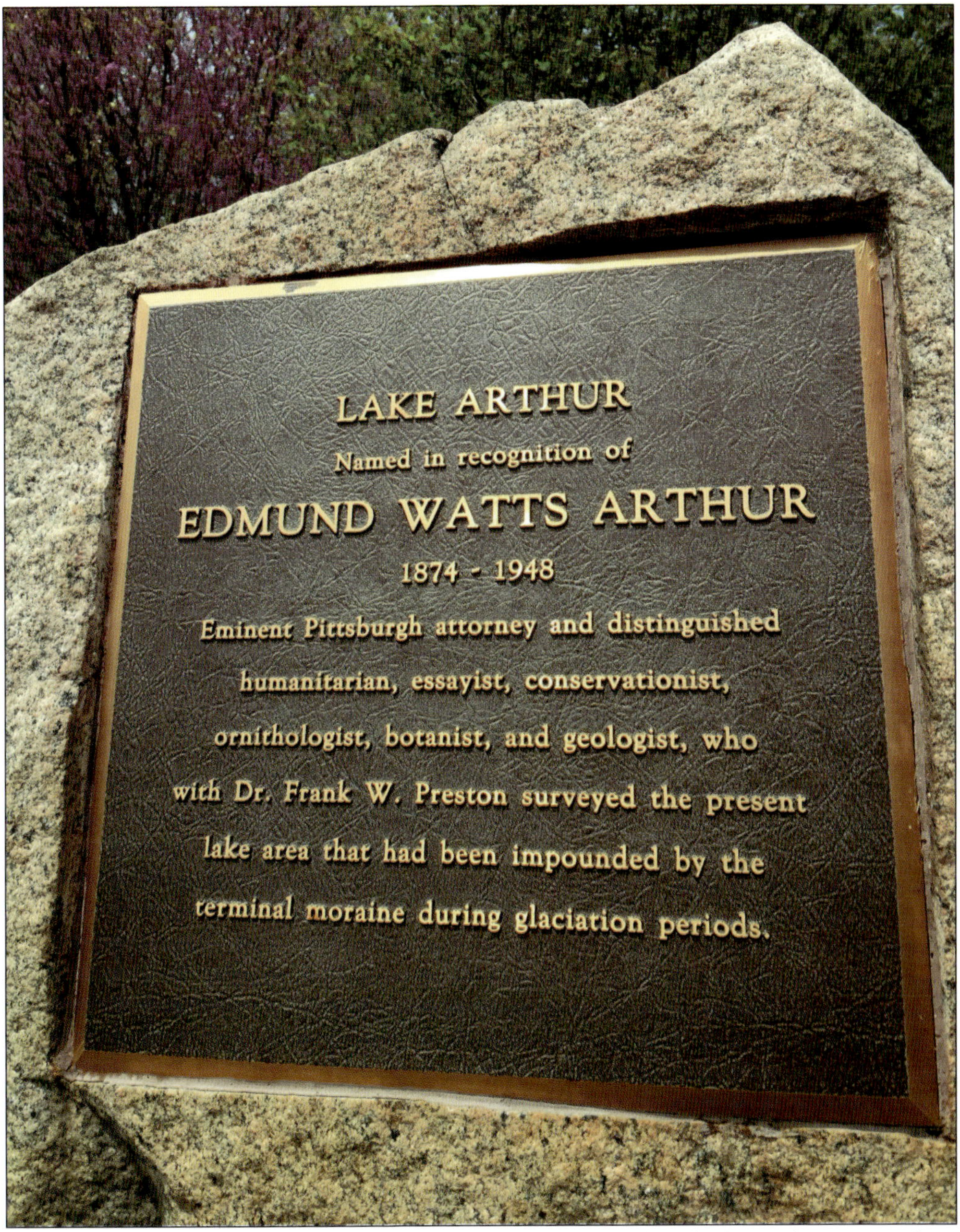

Dr. Preston presented Edmund Watts Arthur's hammer to Paul Feather, the first park superintendent, with directions to row out into the center of the lake and "cast this hammer forth, to claim the lake forever for Arthur." Nancy Wallace, granddaughter of Ned Arthur, especially remembers the dedication ceremony and pondered with her family if an arm would actually reach up for the hammer. It was a memorable day all around. This fitting memorial tribute to Edmund Watts Arthur is mounted outside the park office. The plaque's text includes recognition of his life as an "eminent Pittsburgh attorney and distinguished humanitarian, essayist, conservationist, ornithologist, botanist, and geologist." It is fitting that this wonderful lake be named in memory of him. (Author's collection.)

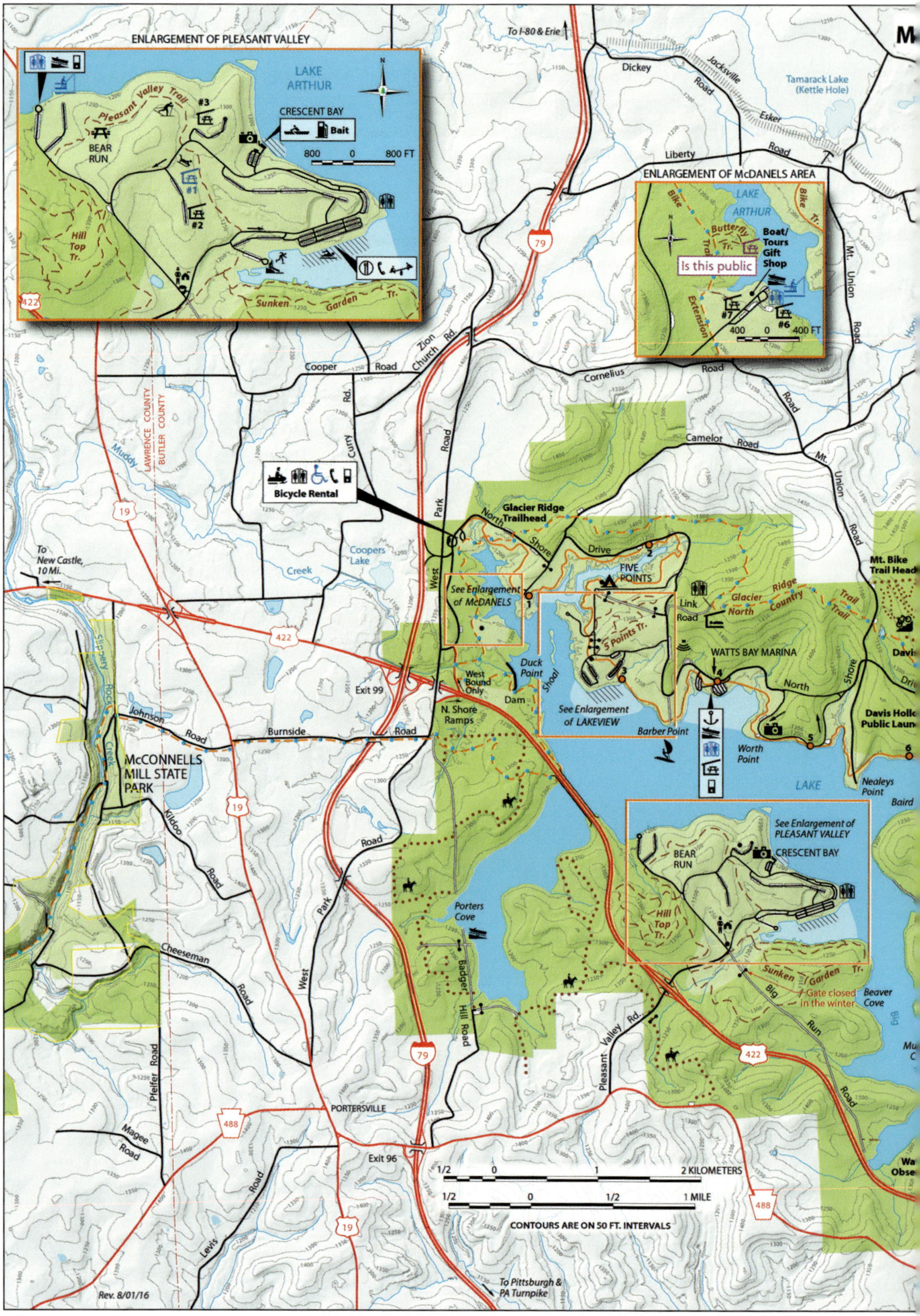

The Pennsylvania Department of Conservation and Natural Resources publishes maps that are available for free at park offices and through the DCNR website or on an app, The Official PA

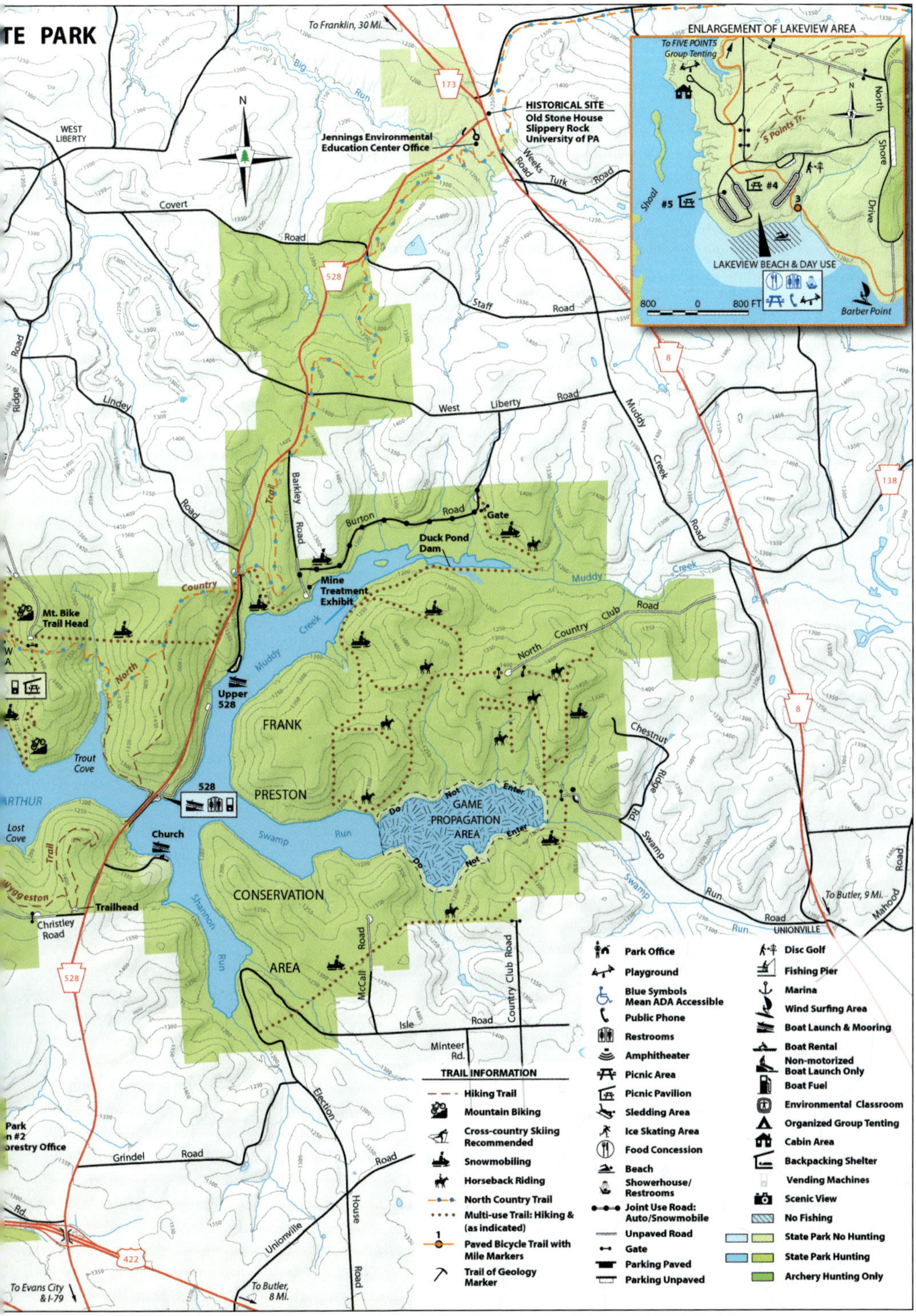

State Park and Forests Park Ranger. This map illustrates Moraine State Park.

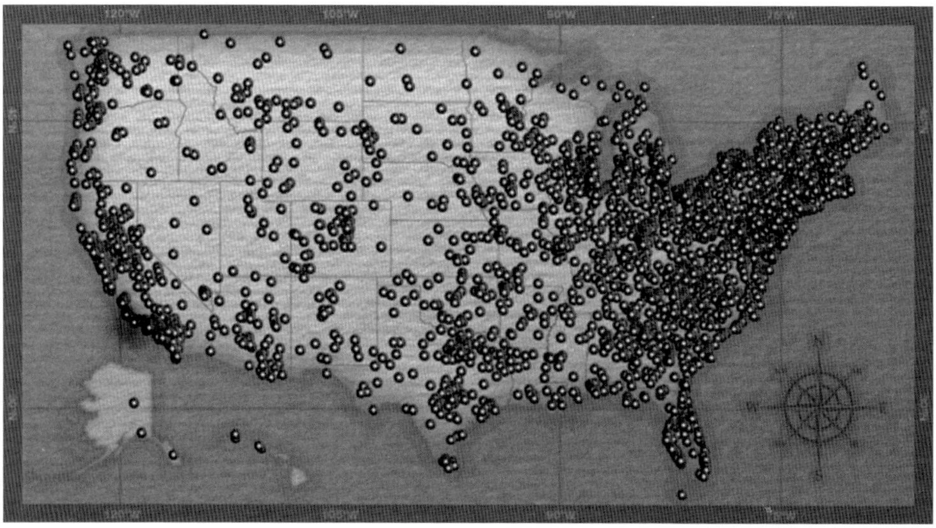